GET A
LIFE!

Other great books for you to get your hands on

Anita Naik
The Just Seventeen Quiz Book
Find out all about yourself, your life and your future by answering the questions in these brilliant quizzes

Am I Normal?
Anita, *Just Seventeen's* amazing agony aunt, answers all those questions you've been too embarrassed to ask

Is This Love?
A guide to the ups and downs of teenage relationships, from flirting and first dates to jealousy and break-ups

Families: Can't Live with Them, Can't Live Without Them!
Whether your problem's overprotective parents, family break-up or a brother from hell, Anita shows that getting along with your family may be easier than you think!

Charlotte Owen
Everything You Ever Wanted To Know About Periods... but didn't like to ask!
All the facts and heaps of really useful advice on this important part of every teenage girl's life. Recommended by the Brook Advisory Centres

Adele Lovell
The Just Seventeen Guide To Being Gorgeous
Want to know how to make the most of what you've got? Adele gives the low-down on hair, skin, make-up, healthy eating and much more

GET A LIFE!

by
Victoria McCarthy

illustrations by Louise Hopkinson

Hodder
Children's
Books

FOR LOUISA — WHOSE LIFE
BRIGHTENED UP SO MANY OTHERS.
WITH LOVE TO ANITA, FOR BEING
ANITA.

Text copyright © 1996 Victoria McCarthy

The right of Victoria McCarthy to be identified as the author of the work has been asserted by her in accordance with the Copyright, Designs and Patents Act 1988.

Illustrations copyright © 1996 Louise Hopkinson

Design by Trisha Mitchell Vargas

Published by Hodder Children's Books 1996

10 9 8 7 6 5 4 3 2

A catalogue record for this book is available from the British Library.

ISBN 0 340 651334

Printed by The Guernsey Press Co. Ltd, Vale, Guernsey, C.I.

Hodder Children's Books
A division of Hodder Headline
338 Euston Road
London NW1 3BH

Contents

ALL ABOUT VICTORIA

Victoria (Vici to those who have bought this book) McCarthy was born on 25 July 1971 in Hartlepool — great place, bad football team. After a stonking academic career with only one claim to fame, that of playing Madonna (the singing one, of course) in the school play, she forayed into the world of journalism. Scoop McCarthy netting a reporter's job on the *Hartlepool Evening Mail*. A year or so later she upped-sticks and moved to London to spend two years and two months working on *Just Seventeen*.

Victoria has since gone freelance (read: turned layabout) and has written two books and penned thousands of words for magazines, including *The Sunday People, Sky, The Clothes Show, Top of The Pops, Ikon* and *Pig Farmer's Weekly*. Now, at the age of 24, Victoria is shunning the glitz of London life and retiring to a village on the west coast of Mexico. There she will while away the day writing children's books and dancing the macarena with her Mexican heart throb.

P.S. Her mum doesn't know about the last part. Tsk, tsk.

LIVE YOUR LIFE, BE FREE!

Life is full of choices — some good, some bad, and a handful that are downright life-threatening. The important thing about having choices is that you can decide what you want and then go for it. You can make and break the rules, go against conventional wisdom and shun a steady 9 to 5 job, or you can aim to be a high-flyer running your own business. That's what choice and getting a life are all about.

Alternatively, you can shrug your shoulders and amble aimlessly through life (though in your case it might just be a shopping centre) in the hope that something good will come your way. But what if a golden opportunity is not waiting for you at the shops or lurking in the innards of your vid? What are you going to do? You could panic. You could ask for help. You could blame society for giving you a raw deal. You could become tea lady for Princess Di. Now that would be very SAAAAD!

Or you could keep reading this book and take some time to meditate on what it's saying, answer the questions and fill-in the filly-in bits. (Don't be afraid to write in this book, it's intended to be used as a workbook.) You'll find advice on friendships and family, attitude adjusting, getting active, getting romantic and generally becoming an all-round happening kind of human. Decide on the changes you want to make in your life and then — most importantly — act on them!

Before you know it you will be happier, your body will be healthier and your mind will expand to extraordinary levels (watch out David Copperfield!). Friends won't recognise the dynamic new you, parents will rush to help, strangers will stop you in the street and ask where you found such awesome inspiration, and rock stars will fall at your feet and want to know your secrets of organisation. And when this happens you'll probably become really smug about it, and everyone will hate you. Still, you can't have everything.

There will in fact be good reasons for feeling at least a little smug because YOU will have made it all happen. This book can help you to change your life by giving you some ideas, but it can't make it a reality — only you can do that.

So go ahead, read and enjoy. If you want your life to improve, it will! Your future is in your hands. May the fun go with you.

Vici

chapter 1

THE LIFE YOU'RE LEAVING

THE ROTTING SYNDROME

No, the rotting syndrome is not a new grunge group and neither is it eligible for treatment on the NHS. This debilitating disease hits kids in the prime of life, turning bright young things into lifeless losers. SHAME! So you don't confuse the rotting syndrome with mould growing on stale bread, or lifeless losers with the recently departed, here's a spotters' guide (no anorak needed). A lifeless loser is a person (well, almost) who:

✦ needs an Ordnance Survey map to get from the sitting room to the front door;

❱ has a complexion a vampire would envy;

✦ knows how many bumps there are on the ceiling above their bed and has given each one a name. Sleep? This bod hibernates!

❱ can recite by heart, and in order, all television

programmes on all stations including cable and satellite;

✦ will watch a television programme even though they know it is utter rubbish;

◗ assume there is nothing exciting to do in their town, despite having only visited it once to get a battery for the remote control. Otherwise they venture out only when legally required — to go to school;

✦ eats, but only during commercial breaks; and

◗ has never even dreamt of the ace life they could be leading.

How, you ask, can these people stand being alone all the time? Ah! but they're not. Lifeless losers have friends, and lots of them. Often, as many as ten can be found, huddling together in front of the television set, eyes glazed and expressions fixed. These poor dears do have families, but they prefer the sparkling stimulation of Teletext.

TRUE CONFESSIONS — MY LIFE WAS AS EXCITING AS A MUG OF LUKEWARM COCOA

Not long ago I, Vici McCarthy, was included in their number. Yes, I was a lifeless loser, a couch potato, suffering from the rotting syndrome. It was a horrible, horrible life.

I worked. I ate. I slept. I snored. But mainly I got bored. Getting bored was the only exercise I did. Even my cat Slouch found my way of life too slow and eventually sought action in the fast lane with a slug. Well, at least it moved.

When Slouch left I realised it was time to do something. Know what I discovered? Hundreds, perhaps even thousands, of similar saddos afflicted with the same condition. Their brains were withering. They were becoming monosyllabic. The biggest word in their vocabulary was 's'boring'. Did they know anything about life's choices? Only as far as they related to prowling the airwaves.

"It's obvious what the problem is," said my friend, pretending to be a psychologist. "You don't have a life."

She was right. I was part of a generation who had become slackers. And you know what is really annoying? It need never have happened. I could have stopped it.

WHY PEOPLE BECOME LIFELESS LOSERS

Lifelessness is usually caused by tiredness, illness, something really depressing happening (which makes you think life's a bummer) or simply falling victim to game shows and soaps.

This is how it happens: because of one of the above reasons, a relatively normal, healthy person spends a week or so doing nothing. They don't see any friends and they don't step outside the front door. Instead, they sit around at home being a dustball — in other words, they lurk in dark corners and are hard to budge. The dustball soon sees that this low-maintenance lifestyle is relaxing and involves absolutely no effort, so they stay put. Double SAAAAD.

One day the dustball realises that all this sitting around and doing bog-all is not providing any emotional satisfaction — like there's no happiness, no laughs, no camaraderie.

The dustball knows that something's missing. It just can't figure out what. Has it missed *Neighbours*? Dinner? Christmas? "Nah," it says, "saw it, ate it, unwrapped it." Then it dawns on the dustball: it's missing a life.

AH, DON'T STOP VICI, WHAT HAPPENS NOW? DOES THE VACUUM CLEANER OF LIFE SUCK THEM UP?

Well, sort of, but it can take time. Let me tell you what happened to me. I went to Brighton to interview some people at a windsurfing championship and everyone was tanned, enthusiastic and having a whale of a time. I, on the other hand, was the colour of frozen milk, able only to harness enough energy to continue breathing and hadn't so much as tittered in a fortnight.

I was shocked. I was embarrassed. I was envious. But more than anything, I wanted to hang out with these people. So I did something about it — I got my act together and pulled myself off the dust heap. And the very first thing I did was look at the pathetic state of my so-called life.

So here's what you have to do: have a look at this very psychological quiz, answer the quick and easy questions and then check out the conclusions.

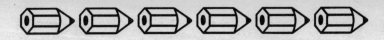

FILL THIS IN!

(Circle the answer that comes closest to your lifestyle)

DO YOU LACK A LIFE?

1 How much TV do you watch a week?

(a) Oh, about two hours on school nights and three or four on Saturdays and Sundays.

(b) Enough. I mean, I watch my favourite shows, but I'm not into channel flicking.

c TV is my friend. I keep it on for its conversational input. God bless the TV.

2 What does fresh air smell like?

(a) It depends. On a really hot day it smells of grass and salt, and on a wet day it smells of, well, it's like this musty smell. But sometimes it smells of hot dogs smothered in chilli, and I have never quite worked out why.

b Fresh air? It doesn't smell of anything, does it? Isn't air, like odourless?

c Got any easier questions?

3 How often do you go places or actually have fun with your friends?

a Every day. We're in loads of the cooler school societies and we go around together all the time.

b At school we do things, I guess. On Saturdays we hang out in the shopping centre.

c Friends?

4 Did you see that episode of *Brookside* when Sinbad the window cleaner lost his bucket?

a Yeah. Brilliant wasn't it? But not as good as the time Jackie Corkhill found a button in her pizza.

b Er...no. Sinbad off *Brookside* never lost his bucket. You're thinking of the time Bet Lynch stood in one on *Coronation Street*.

c Nup. I was probably bungee jumping or abseiling in Cheddar Gorge that day.

5 What's your ten-point strategy towards a promising future in relation to the social and economic aspects of your life?

a Erm, if you mean "how do I see my future?", I don't. I haven't a clue what I want to do. Should I?

b Dunno. I've got a pretty good idea of what I want out of life, but I'm not really doing much about it yet.

c Could you repeat the question?

6 You create your own destiny. True or false?

a True. Unfortunately, I seem to be creating a life which revolves around *Roseanne*, Pot Noodles and the school yard. Help! I need you Vici.

b False. I'd love to be a Hollywood movie producer, but I don't hear Quentin Tarantino knocking on my door.

c Don't know. Don't care. Next!

7 Which of the following most accurately describes your love life:

a Nobody loves me, everybody hates me, I'm going to eat some worms.

b I don't have romance 'cos I never meet anyone interesting. The only potential love interest lives next door, and he keeps dead terrapins. I mean, really...

c It happens in fits and starts, but basically I'm not fit to be snogged.

8 Tick which of these activities you have done recently:

Had a midnight picnic ☐

Snowboarded, surfed, bodyboarded or got wet somewhere other than in the shower ☐

Gone on a trip with your mates ☑

Written letters to people whose jobs you might like to do ☐

Had a sorting and organising session ☐
Gone off somewhere to think ☑
Read a book ☑
Turned off the TV because there was something much better to do, or because the TV was pumping out rubbish ☑
Laughed till you cried ☑
Rearranged the furniture in the lounge to get a clearer view of the box ☐

9 What have you got to offer society?

a 3p and half a packet of Polos.

b My potential. (Wicked answer!)

c Nothing. I'm no good at anything. I'm absolutely useless.

10 A man has a box. It is a black box. He loves the box. What do you reckon?

a He's a nutter. Anyone who loves a black box needs to see more of the world.

b The black box probably reminds him of a brilliant day he had snowboarding with his chums or something. However, I reckon he should not dwell on his black box, but go out and have more life-enriching experiences.

c Life is like a black box. It's dark and a bit square (or is that cuboid?). I'm with the man on this one.

Now, add up...

...your scores

1) a-1; b-2; c-0.

2) a-2; b-1; c-0.

3) a-2; b-1; c- minus 312

4) a-0; b-1; c-2 plus 264 for braveness.

5) a-1; b-2; c-0.

6) a-2; b-1; c-minus heaps.

7) a-0; b-2; c-1.

8) One point for each option except the last one. Deduct 5 points from your score for rearranging the furniture.

9) a-1; b-2; c-0.

10) a-1; b-2; c-0.

How does your life rate?

If you scored 19-293, you have a life, but...

You seem to be pretty well-adjusted. Your life is on an even keel and you have worked out a balance between work and play. You don't watch too much TV and you get up off your bum and do things. Most importantly you know that you are the master of your own future, however even you can't resist the temptation to pot-noodle your way through *Roseanne.* Be on your guard for these time-wasting life suckers. As you are already well on the way to a rip-roaring, satisfying life, everything else you do will be icing on the cake. So read on, the chocolate sprinkles and glacé cherry are just around the corner.

A score of 11-18 means you're breathing, but only just Hmm, you're about normal. You have potential to be a life-getter, but there's also a chance of slipping into dustball hell. Maybe you need to find a couple of extra out-of-school activities to broaden your horizons. Reading *Get a Life!* will, of course, make all the difference to your cooler future.

If you scored 10 or below send for an ambulance, now Oh dear, we might have come a bit late. You're AWOL — an adolescent without life. Still, the *Get A Life!* paramedics are here, and with the aid of this manual you will find it easy to escape your current abysmal status of suburban burn-out, and become a Colossus. What's a Colossus? A hugely important person, of course.

Now that's done, we can get on with the real business. Adios to the life we're leaving, and hola! to the life we're going to live. Use the following diary, and the ones you'll find at the end of every chapter, to review your life-getting progress over the next three months. Answer the questions and get literary satisfaction.

If you're worried about domestic sneaks taking peaks at your diary, photocopy the cover of a book that no-one in their right mind would voluntarily choose to read (for example, a maths book or computer manual) and wrap it around the irresistibly seductive *Get A Life!* cover. Your secret thoughts are now safe. Tee hee.

My Diary
JUST THE FACTS

Name: Alex

Age: 11

Greatest passions:

To be a vet, or be a
vetterinre nurse

Greatest peeves:

Life happiness rating: circle 0 if nothing has made you smile recently; score 10 if you're over-the-moon about everything.

0   1   2   3   4   5   6   7   8   (9)   10

Having gone through chapter 1, what do you feel you need to change in your life? Socks, knickers and shampoo/conditioner are not valid answers.

This month:

To change attarjude to friends

Month 2: To change my attarjide
troavars my family

Month 3: Have more fun

chapter 2

WHAT KIND OF LIFE DO YOU WANT?

ONLY POSITIVE, UPBEAT ANSWERS, PLEASE

At this point you can either let the vacuum cleaner of life suck you in and allow it to control your destiny, or you can take a stand and carve out the kind of life you really want. I know it's hard to believe but some folks actually let tea leaves, glass balls, playing cards and all manner of fortune-telling paraphernalia tell them what to do. Instead of taking control of their lives and trying to achieve all the things they dream about, these people pay £20 to a woman with her head wrapped in a tea-towel.

They let themselves be told that their future has already been decided and there's zippidy-do they can do to change it. Baloney! You've got choices — and lots of them.

SWEET DREAMS

What we're going to do now is close our eyes and daydream about what we want our lives to be like, about how we'd like to live and what we want to do. Then we will be able to work out how to turn our dreams into reality. By the end of this chapter you'll hopefully realise that if you can dream it, you can do it!

The only words of advice I have to offer are that on no account should you confuse your dreams with the lifestyle images portrayed in glossy mags. You know the type: movie stars and sportspeople lounging around in their £3m French farmhouses, pedigree dogs curled up beside them, dozens of sleek cars parked on the drive and enough lucrative deals going down to pay off the gross national debt of Nicaragua.

Understandably you might envy their cool life, but is it what you really want? Are you willing to live for six months of the year in a caravan on location? Do you want to get up at dawn every morning to run 20 kilometres, then lift weights for the rest of the day? Successful and fulfilling lives come in many guises so try to create your own, not borrow someone else's.

Something to do

Find somewhere comfortable, quiet and private. Close your eyes, relax and allow yourself 30 minutes of quality dream time.

To help you get started, think about these questions

✦ Where would you be living?
▶ What hobbies would you have?
✦ Would you be married or single?
▶ Would you have children?
✦ Do you want the simple life or do you hanker for possessions?

Don't worry about the exact job you want, and don't try to come up with really long-term plans to make your dream come true. They may look so daunting that you'll

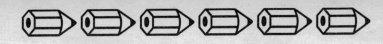

FILL IT IN!

WRITE DOWN YOUR DREAM LIFESTYLE

dump the whole project on the too-hard pile. While you're dreaming this book will pump out some relaxing vibes. When you're ready fill-in the filly in bit opposite.

As you read *Get A Life!* replay your dream to keep you on the right track. You may even want to rewrite your dream. On my thirteenth birthday I wanted to spend my life horse-riding. A week later, after mucking out the stables, horse-riding was the stuff of nightmares. My new dream was to ride the waves. Isn't having choices just grand?

IT'S A GOOOOOOAAAAL!

This dream is now your goal. A goal is a specific task you wish to achieve, and so that you can check if you're on course to fulfil it, set yourself some time limits. If your goal is open-ended, it's ever so easy to put it off, saying "I'll do it tomorrow."

Believe it or not, you and Ryan Giggs have more in common than a love of *Coronation Street* and an affinity for buttered popcorn — you both have goals.

Granted, Ryan's are a little more obvious than yours. He is focused on knocking a leather ball past a couple of blokes and a goalkeeper into a large shopping basket. Your goals, however, are a tad more general and certainly more important. Ryan might save his team from relegation by putting one in the net, but your goals will save you from relegation to life's 3rd Division.

Let's say the ball represents your life and that your

passing, kicking, heading and dribbling techniques are strategies for achieving your goals. Using these skills, you manoeuvre the ball into your net and score a goal, an achievement which helps you to develop your life and gives you the chance to play yet more games.

With every goal scored you move closer to claiming the ultimate trophy — the FA Cup of your dream life.

WHY GOALS ARE TRÈS IMPORTANT

Goals are to life what jam is to peanut butter: you really shouldn't have one without the other. (What? You've never tried a jam and peanut butter sarnie? Where have you been?) There is research by the tonne which proves that people who set themselves goals are much more likely to succeed in every area of their life. And to make the job easier, these goal-getters break down their grand dreams into smaller, more manageable short-term ones.

Let's say you want to improve your French because one of your goals is to be an animal rights activist hassling French farmers over their practice of raising calves in crates. Your short-term goal and time limit might be to learn a table of irregular verbs by the end of the week. This is a realistic goal. (An unrealistic one would be expecting yourself to read Napoleon's diaries by tea-time.) When you've mastered your list of irregular verbs, you've put one in the net and come closer to making the world a nicer place. Simple, oui?

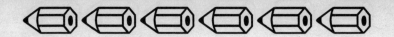

Something to do and fill-in

To get used to all this goal-setting business, why don't you assist 15-year-old Mildred de Glamour (cool name) work out hers? This little bit of practice will help you to be objective and logical when you come to planning your own goal-shooting strategy.

Mildred de Glamour of 17 Bonaverage Drive has decided it would be brilliant to be a charity development worker in South America. To do this Mildred will have to learn Spanish, and then go on to master the Castilian pronunciation as used in Latin America. It would also be a good idea for Mildred to get some experience of working with a charity. She has also realised that a university qualification in a Third World development subject would also be an asset. So what does Mildred need to do?

Goal sheet for Mildred De Glamour

Super goal To be a charity development worker in South America by the time she's 22!

Goal 1 To be fluent in Spanish within 3 years.

Sub goal Find an affordable tutor within a month.
Sub goal Learn beginner's Spanish within a year.
Sub goal Learn advanced Spanish within two years.
Sub goal Learn Castilian at a Latin American institute.

Goal 2 To get work experience with a charitable organisation over the next 12 months. (Fill in the blanks and get Mildred on her way.)
Sub goal
Sub goal
Sub goal

Goal 3 To receive a Third World Development university qualification by the time I'm 21.
Sub goal Within a month, see a careers counsellor to find out about careers which suit my interests, and also ask about the qualifications needed.
Sub goal Within two months, write to the universities and ask what I need to qualify for those courses.
Sub goal Decide which subjects I need to study at school, and work hard to get brilliant exam marks.

Get the idea? Now fill in your own goal-shooting diary on page 10.

IT DOESN'T MATTER IF YOU DON'T SCORE EVERY TIME

It would be lovely if you achieved every goal you ever set, but life's not that simple. For a start, you may change your mind about what you want to do. Secondly, changes in your home life or extra pressure at school may mean putting a goal on hold. And finally, you may have to rethink the whole plan if circumstances beyond your control make that goal impossible.For example, university course pre-requisites may alter, or job opportunities disappear.

I had a friend who wanted to be in the diplomatic service. She was offered a job in the foreign office on the condition that she completed her degree, but a sudden change in government policy stopped diplomatic recruitment. This meant that the career she wanted was no longer feasible, but it didn't stop her continuing at uni. She just sussed out some new goals. So don't throw in the towel and leave the field in a huff if everything doesn't go exactly to plan.

The important thing about goal-setting is that it sets the ball in motion, and even if you have to change strategy you've got to keep the ball moving.

Lighten up

You've still got plenty of time, so there's no need to make all the mega-life decisions now. I can name hundreds of scientists, actors, ecologists, business people and teachers who didn't get into their professions until they were in their 30s. So don't panic if you're not 100 per cent sure of your life's goals. To find out more about careers and study, read chapter 9.

My Diary
My Goal Sheet

Super goal:
....
In order to achieve my super goal, I have to do the following:

Goal 1:
....
Sub goal: ....
Sub goal: ....
Sub goal: ....

Goal 2:
....
Sub goal: ....
Sub goal: ....
Sub goal: ....

Goal 3:
....
Sub goal: ....
Sub goal: ....
Sub goal: ....

Note here any changes to your lifestyle dreams, and work out how you are going to achieve your new goals.

This month: ....
....
....

Month 2: ....
....
....

Month 3: ....
....
....

chapter 3

LIFE CHANGES THAT TAKE MINUTES

LET'S GET SPEEDY FOR THE NEEDY

No, I'm not joking. It *really* is possible to make some simple, positive changes to your life in just a few minutes. Make-overs for misfits will, unfortunately, take a little longer, so don't expect instant miracles. Life, after all, is not a container of dehydrated noodle that only requires boiling water to turn it instantly into a meal. Let's say you want to give your bedroom a new look. You could rip off the old wallpaper, renew the windows, plaster the ceiling, rewire the electrics, and lay new carpet. Now that's a big, big job. Agree?

Alternatively, you could simply clean the windows, wash your curtains, rearrange the furniture, put up some new posters and buy a rug to cover the chunderous carpet. In just a couple of hours you've given your bedroom a new lease of life. You now feel better about your bedroom, and doubly inspired to get down and tackle a major decorating job.

The same is true of life-tweaking. In this chapter we're going to give the fixtures and fittings of your life a make-over, and show you some things you can do now (like today) to make your life much cooler.

THE 60-MINUTE MAKE-OVER

1 Smile

Think this is lame? Think this is just too simple to make any real difference to your life? Well, listen-up, buster — you're wrong.

SOMETHING TO DO

Try to make yourself cry. (If your happiness rating in chapter 1 was 0, then just continue crying.) When you cry your posture slumps and your shoulders become rounded. You'll get a sinking feeling in the pit of your stomach and your mascara will run (yuk!). A bout of the down-in-the-dumps is on its way. All this happens because your brain automatically associates crying with sadness. And the symptoms of sadness exhibit themselves not only emotionally, but physically.

Being happy and smiling works in the same way. When you're happy your brain tells the face muscles to pucker up at the corners of your mouth so you grin rather inanely. At the same time your brain releases 'happy' hormones which instantly lift your spirits and make you more attractive. And you know what that means.

See? It's that easy: smile and your brain smiles with you! Next time you're walking down a busy street or into a crowded room, let your face do the grin thing (but don't go overboard, people might think you're one slice short of a loaf). Notice how people want to talk to you? Count the number of smiles you receive in return? Weird, huh? Smiling is a people-catcher so don't mock it, use it!

D.I.N.

can be used anywhere, at any time.

It's the perfect solution to all those everyday problems.

★ **Grass stains on your PE shorts?**
Wash them now!

★ **Maths test next week?**
Start revising now!

★ **Had a tiff with your mum?**
Sort it out now!

Using D.I.N. will change your life!

Family and friends won't recognise the new you!

D.I.N. will never let you down and comes with a life-time guarantee.

D.I.N. is available now at all good stockists.

2 Do it now

This is my least favourite life-changer. Because I was a
born slacker — why do it today, when there's always
next week? — it took me ages to get a handle on the
'do it now' (D.I.N.) technique, but once I mastered it my
life improved tenfold.

**The D.I.N. trick is simple: don't put off till
tomorrow what you can do now.**

You've got a long-term school project to do? Start it
now and you'll have more time to research and write it
up. You'll be able to stagger the workload, so that you
can squeeze in some highly-desirable socialising. If
you slack off and don't start the project till the day
before the deadline, you'll (a) panic and hand in
rubbish; (b) do half a job and still hand in rubbish or, (c)
come up with an excuse that your teacher will
recognise is rubbish. For those who are poor at multiple
choice: a, b and c are all bad moves.

3 Turn off the TV...and D.I.N!

How many times have you sat zombified in front of the
box thinking: "Maan, this is boring. Why don't they
make good TV any more?" Too often, is my guess. Most
TV is rubbish, so why watch it? You know you could be
doing something better: going out with your mates,
reading, writing a letter or even studying (in which case
you'll have free time when you really need it — like
when the hunk in history asks you to go ice skating).

Turning off the TV set now, doesn't mean turning it off forever. It just means being selective — making choices — about what you watch. I can't live without *Soldier Soldier* (it's a highlight of my week. Sad, right?) and a week without *Brookside* would probably make me cry. If you really want to watch a programme, fine. If not, turn it off. You're wasting precious time.

4 Be nice to people

Being nice to people might seem a bit wet and worthy, but it's actually quite a self-help thing to do. If you're nice to your mamaaah, she'll be less likely to hassle

 you about your clothes. If you're sweet to your sister, she'll freak out and go crazy (and won't that be fun?). I've heard that teachers and others in positions of authority also respond well to a dose of nice-ness. Don't confuse

being nice with grovelling. One involves being pleasant and good, the other means sacrificing your self-esteem. Patching up your differences with people (and D.I.N.) will make you happy and give you an all-round easier time.

It's very difficult to have a positive outlook on life if you wake up in the morning just to have the usual daily row with your brother. Your life will improve dramatically if you wipe the slate clean, and clear up old arguments. Apologise for being a grouch (even if you think you shouldn't have to), and make an effort to sort out grumbles before they escalate into grudges. Having a peaceful, happy home life will lay strong foundations for your life in the outside world. For more tips on dealing with your family see chapter 7.

5 Stop the sulks

Me? Sulk? I sulk big-time. Flatmate's been in the bath for half an hour, I sulk. A story I'm writing doesn't work, major sulk. Best friend says she's dating the boy I like, major, monster-raving-rollicking sulk. And you know what it achieves? Absolutely nothing.

I get upset and feel bad for a few hours. Everyone ignores me, and even Slouch retreats into a corner. My mood casts a grey cloud over the entire household. Sulks are just a big waste of time and energy. So life-change number 5 is: stop sulking. Say what you've got to say, but stay calm. Argue your point, but keep cool. Above all, don't sulk! It ain't pretty.

CHANGES THAT WILL TAKE A DAY

1 Organise your space

Your own piece of personal real estate, whether it be a bedroom for one or more, or a tiny nook at the top of the stairs, it is where you'll spend the bulk of your time. You might do your homework there, use it for entertaining friends, or just as a bolt-hole to get away from the family, but one thing's for sure — your personal space affects your ability to think and work.

If you try to work in a messy bedroom, you'll get confused and spend eons looking for vital stuff. And if you have to clear space on your desk before you can actually sit down and start anything, you'll be put off the whole project.

For ages my room was such a tip I used to do my work crouching in the hall. In winter, I had to wear coat and gloves because the wind that whistled under the front door was sub-zero. In summer, when the front door was left open, every passer-by got a good view of my cleavage.

Working in the hall was not ideal, but in comparison to my room (lovingly called the 'skip' because I used to throw junk into it), the hall was paradise. If only I had spent a day or so organising my room I could have saved myself a lot of back pain, colds and pervy looks. I would have also found my fave shirt I thought I'd lost.

So sort your room and D.I.N. Go overboard and personalise your stuff: decorate pots to hold pencils and use boxes to safeguard treasures. Use your ingenuity and make shelf files out of trimmed cereal containers, and drawers from old shoe boxes.

2 Get your work in order

Messy and disorganised notes make hard work of studying, and tend to freak teachers out. I know it's environmentally-motivated, but covering every square millimetre of a sheet of paper (recycled, of course) with tiny writing is really taking things too far. Make your notes a joy to behold; lash out with colours and replace verbiage with diagrams. Don't attempt to titivate all your work in one sitting. Do it one subject at a time and you'll find that it will become a revision session. So, when it comes to a spot test, it'll seem like cool surf!

3 Make some fun!

Fun doesn't just happen. It happens when someone extracts a digit and makes it happen. Granted, there's the odd occasion when fun makes a surprise appearance, but you can't count on it. Chances are, the mega-frolics won't erupt in the shopping centre.

Fun results when you put some effort into planning a day trip, organising a party, playing in a band or choreographing your own synchronised water ballet (Don't forget your nose clips!)

Good times materialise when you phone up your mates and scheme to have a good time. So why not get on the blower and organise a few days of veritable fun-ness? If you're stuck for ideas, flip to pages 61-69.

4 Relax... just like, chill, maan!

Relaxing might seem like a ridiculous thing to do when you're trying to get a more happening life, but it's actually way, way important.

Your brain and your body are like the body and engine of a car (oh no, another Vici simile on the way), but if the car is not serviced and repaired regularly, then it's going to let you down. And you can bet your last penny that it will conk out on the very day you most need it. And what about you? If you work continuously and hard, as you do, say, before an exam, you too will conk out. Your work will be affected, your health in tatters, and your emotions will go on a roller coaster ride you'll never forget. This is why you need to give your body down-time (sleep), and your brain time-off for good behaviour. Relaxing and resting does not mean going totally zombie. A walk in the woods or listening to some gentle music will do the trick. Chapter 4 contains info on meditation and general chilling-out. Read it and use it. You'll see improvement immediately.

5 Do some life-branching

Life-branching is a pen and paper method of working out life changes for a groovier time. It's really just a

disguised word association game, minus the probing white-coated psychologist.

Get a huge sheet of paper and, in the middle, write the name of a subject which is on your mind (for example, it could be maths because you've got a test coming up). Draw radiating lines from the word, and at the end of each line write a word associated with the topic. For maths you might include the name of the teacher and some formulae. Then from each of those words, draw more lines and write other associations. Keep on doing this — drawing more branches and adding more words until you fill the page. Once you've done that, look at each of the words you've written and ask yourself how they affect you. If a word sends shivers down your spine, write that word on another page and see if you can work out a way to improve your knowledge of it, or minimise your anxiety about it. Start drawing lines from this word and writing down associated words. Do this for every item that causes you grief. When you come up with solutions, write those on a separate piece of paper; this list becomes your job sheet. For example, your mission might be: "Don't be scared of Miss Goodman, and practise algebra".

Life-branching helps you sort out the stuff you know or aren't worried about, from the grit that's getting you down. Go on, try it.

There you have it — ten small things you can do to make huge changes in your life. So far so good. Now what? Er...how about some serious attitude adjusting?

My Diary
Life's little make-overs

Tick those instant life-changes that you found the most helpful:

O Smiling

☐ Doing it now (D.I.N.)

O Turning off the TV

☐ Being nice to people

O Stopping the sulks

☐ Organising your space

O Getting your work in order

☐ Making some fun

O Relaxing

☐ Life-branching

Write down your own ideas for other instant life changes which you are going to try:

This month:
....
....
....

Month 2:
....
....
....

Month 3:
....
....
....

chapter 4

IT'S ALL A MATTER OF ATTITUDE

HOW TO GET THOSE POSITIVE FEELINGS

A few years ago I went to America to interview a female rock musician. Just as I was due to leave my hotel to meet the celeb, I got a phone call from her frantic publicist who said she just had to talk to me. The celeb, it seemed, had had an awful week. She'd lost a part she'd desperately wanted in a movie, had been slagged off in the press, and, to top it all, her mum wasn't very well. The publicist was frank (well, Sue actually): "She's tired and obviously a bit down," she said. "If she gets upset we might have to postpone the interview." An hour later I turned up at the celeb's house expecting to be told to leave, or at best to meet a grumpy, sullen rock star, but no. She was friendly, polite, happy, enthusiastic and quite positive, even when I asked her about the slagging-off she'd received. Later I confided to her that I was surprised at her demeanour towards me, given the week she'd had. "Well," she said, shrugging, "it's all a question of attitude."

Never was a truer word spoken. If you want to improve your life in a deep and meaningful way, you've got to get your attitude in line. If a low mark on a test sends your confidence plummeting or a knock-back on the love front makes you cry for months, then you need to change — or at least fine-tune — the way you think. You need to think positively.

GAAH, LIFE'S POOP

It's all too easy to think that and be miserable. You turn on the TV and the news is full of gloom: your friends and relatives are unemployed, everyone's going on

about the earth warming up, species disappearing, and children trapped in war zones. Ugh! it's all too much. What's there to be positive about?

Y'see, if that's the attitude you decide to take, doom city is your destination. You're only looking at the dark side of things, the bad news.

HAVE I GOT GOOD NEWS FOR YOU!

Countries once at war are becoming allies. Cures are being found for diseases. Discoveries are being made that will improve life forever. Your future, and that of your family and friends and the world in general, can be changed by you! You can help someone less fortunate. You can help stamp out racism. Endangered animals and their environment can be saved. You can develop true friendships, fall in love, and experience all of life's pleasures. But only if you can see the possibilities.

For instance, if it's raining and you think, "Yuk, I'm going to get wet, my new boots will be covered in mud and my hair's going to go berserk" you will, without a shadow of a doubt, be in the dumps. Alternatively, if you say, "Excellent! Great day to show off my new hat" you'll be on a high. Here's are some more examples of how to turn bad news into good:

BAD I'm not allowed out tonight.
GOOD I'll be really rested and look doubly glam tomorrow.

 BAD He doesn't fancy me.
GOOD Yeah, but he has no taste. There are a hundred million boys out there who are cute and know a good thing when they see it.

 BAD My friends have all got boyfriends and I haven't.
GOOD I'm free to do what I want any old time. Tee hee.

 BAD I'm not part of the clique at school.
GOOD I'm too unique to follow a gang that behaves like a flock of sheep. Baaaaa.

 BAD There's nothing to do.
GOOD Here's an opportunity to call up everyone and organise some fun.

 BAD That girl doesn't like me.
GOOD That girl hasn't taken the time to know me. Lots of other people like me.

 BAD I'm rubbish at sports.
GOOD Yeah, but I'm great at maths and art.

 BAD I'll never get a boyfriend like Jenny's.
GOOD No, I'll get a boyfriend better suited to me.

Be positively charged

You can't have a fun-packed, zest-filled happy life unless you have self-esteem and practise self-respect. Self-esteem is really believing in your own worth and potential. For example, knowing that you can be a test pilot if that's what you want. Having self-respect will give you the courage to say 'no' to smoking and drugs, to turn down unwanted sexual advances, and to stand up for issues you believe in, like tolerance and equality. You know you are a great human being and you've got the self-esteem and self-respect to prove it. You're not going to let anyone drag you down. Everyone is made equal and, irrespective of social position, looks or brains, no one is more important than anyone else. Make the most of yourself and you'll show yourself the ultimate respect!

Something to do

Make a list of all your good points and don't stop until you can think of at least 50! Pin the list above your bed or desk, as a constant reminder of your greatness.

Dealing with down-ness

It's not easy to be positive all the time; some things, unfortunately, have no bright side, no silver lining. But by the same token many of us are ace at over-reacting,

FILL IT IN!

Can you recall an instance when your lack of self-esteem stopped you doing something? Write it here.

What should you have done?

Think of three ways in which you can show yourself more respect.

1

2

3

How can you be more in control of your life? Think of two or three things, and write them here.

turning a small set-back into a right-royal retreat. As my mum would say we make mountains out of molehills.

This is what happened to a friend of mine when she failed a test: she felt that she a) was useless, b) would never pass her exams, c) couldn't become an engineer, and d) was convinced her teacher hated her. My mate spent hours worrying about each of these four problems. She even cried.

Know what? It turned out that she'd failed the test because she had misunderstood the meaning of one word in a question. My friend was well-equipped to do well in that test, and there was no way she was going to flunk her exams and fail to be an engineer. Her teacher didn't hate her of course, he sympathised with her disappointment.

My friend had wasted piles of time and made herself desperately unhappy because she over-reacted and lost a grip on her self-esteem. Instead of going to her teacher and finding out what went wrong, she went right in at the deep end and lost all perspective on the problem.

DUMPING THE DUMPS

1 Make sure you know exactly what's getting you down and face up to it.

2 Reason with yourself to make certain you're not over-reacting. Is this hassle really worth all this angst?

3 Try to talk yourself out of being upset. Tell yourself in a stern voice that this hassle is a mere hiccup, and that you will overcome it. So there, take that, you pesky pimple of a problem.

4 Get an objective second opinion from a good bud. Don't become obsessed by telling the story over and over again to every one you know.

5 If you think the problem warrants outside help, then ask for it. Don't let pride or embarrassment hold you back. Confucius say: a problem shared, is halved.

6 And above all, keep calm.

THE MOODY BLUES

Welcome aboard the good ship emotional mood swing. It's a turbulent crossing, this one. Sometimes it rises on the happy crest of a wave and then — kerboom — it dives into deepest and murkiest water imaginable. And you know what's behind all this? Your moods.

All of us know that life can't always be on a high. We sadly accept that bad times are sure to follow hot on the heels of good. By being so pessimistic we open the door and roll out the red carpet to a bad mood. But it doesn't always have to be like this. Try out the ideas on the following pages, and you'll be bolting the door on the moody blues.

Something to do

Keep a diary and as well as recording all the "he said, she said" stuff, give each day a mood rating. The system I use is taken straight off the weather report.

✦ Great mood = sun

◗ So-so mood = sun with cloudy patches

✦ Just the pits = flash of lightning

Keep an eye on your diary and see if there is any pattern in your mood swings. Are they cyclical (say, weekly or monthly)? Do they come immediately before or after a certain event? Are they associated with a particular person? Once you know what affects your mood swings, you can start to control them. For example, if you find that there is one particular nerd who brings you down on a regular basis, learn to take everything they say or do with a pinch of salt. Better still, go out of your way to avoid them.

Your moods are in your hands! (Or should that be your head?)

The chilling-out technique

In chapter 3 I mentioned relaxation and talked about how important it was if you wanted to be a happy, healthy person. Remember? Well, meditation is a brilliant way of learning to think positively and getting to

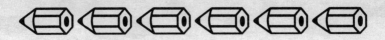

FILL IT IN!

Design your mood symbols and draw them here. Don't forget to write what each one means.

SYMBOL   MOOD

HERE'S SOME WE PREPARED EARLIER.

Top day

Bad start – great finish

pash

Super worker

Just the pits

good people day

Bad people day.

Bad hair day

know the deep-down you. While you're relaxing you can reflect calmly about things you've done, how you've coped (or didn't cope) with problems and how you could handle them better next time. Soooo, welcome to meditation class folks! And by the way, you can forget the white robes and Eastern mantras.

Something to do

Find yourself a comfy chair in a quiet spot, relax and close your eyes (er...after you've read this paragraph, all right?). In your mind, imagine your dream house situated in your favourite landscape (it could be beside a lake, on a tropical island, at the foot of a snow-capped mountain, or whatever). Have a good look at the house from the outside and then enter it. Walk around the house having a nosy. You'll discover that the house has a health room (for use when you're feeling under the weather), a career room (where you try out any job you might like to do), and a library (for filing and retrieving information, including school work). The last room in your house is the relaxation room. Make this room the most beautiful of all.

Other than yourself, there is only one person in your house, and his or her job is to help you and offer advice when you need it. This person can be a friend, a fave musician, a celluloid celeb, or even an alien.

When you need to relax you enter your house and

deal with whatever's on your mind. If you're feeling low, go and lie in the health room, and relax while your helper uses coloured lights to cure you. Use the library to focus your attention on the essay you're about to start. Get the picture?

There are other ways of chilling out, and if you have already sussed the best route for you, then use it. It doesn't matter how you do it, it's just important that your mind is relaxed and healthy. It automatically follows that your attitude will start to buzz with positive vibes.

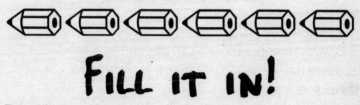

FILL IT IN!

Describe your house and its location.

Who is your chosen assistant?

What did you do in your house today?

My Diary

UPPING THE ATTITUDE

How has your attitude changed this month? For example, you might have had fewer moody days, or solved a problem that's been bugging you for ages.

Month1:
....
....
....
....

Month 2:
....
....
....
....

Month 3:
....
....
....
....

Think of other areas of your life where an attitude change would make things better:

1...
2...
3...
4...
5...

chapter 5

HEY, WANT SOME ENDORPHINS?

THE XTC OF EXERCISE

The turning tide. An action romance from the pen, and heart, of Victoria McCarthy

It was his gaze that attracted my attention. I was drawn by his piercing azure eyes, shining out from under his jaw-length black hair as he stood on the beach at Biarritz in the warm, night-time air. He was staring at the ocean's horizon and listening intently to the waves breaking out on the reef.

"What's wrong?" I asked, thinking that he was one wave short of a set. He didn't reply. His expression remained fixed.

Then I realised that he, the one and only Kelly Slater, was meditating, clearing his mind so that he could focus on his task to be triumphant, yet again, in the World Surfing Championships. Oh, what was I to do, poor slacker me, in the presence of this god?

Until this chance meeting, I was a fully-paid up subscriber to the slacker way of life. I did as little as possible for as long as possible, and then complained about it lots. My life back home revolved around reading D&M (deep and meaningful) novels, going to gigs and eating take-away food. Now all these things are good, but only if they form part of your life, not your whole existence. I may have been well-read and totally up-to-date music-wise, but, believe me, I was miserable. I was in a major mope mood. But in the presence of wave-rider numero uno, I decided it was time to turn the tide of my so-called life around. I didn't want to stop doing all the things that I had been doing, I just wanted to experience new get-up-and-go activities.

DOES YOUR MIND AND BODY NEED SERIOUS CLEANING?

I'd always had a rough idea of how to keep my body and mind running like clockwork but, sadly, I ignored it!
✦ To keep your mind healthy you keep it open by reading and learning.
❯ To keep your body healthy you respect it and give it regular exercise.
✦ To keep both your body and mind pumped up with energy, eat good food.

But there was a final element in the mind and body equation I really hadn't reckoned on — and it's one that Kelly Slater shared with me. Your attitude and emotions are affected by the way you treat your body. You know how you sometimes feel a bit weird and slightly depressed a few days before your period? Well, this pre-menstrual syndrome is basically caused by a stirring of hormones in your body, preparing you for your period. But here's the hub: hormones are affected by your physical health, stress levels, intake of chemicals (for example, alcohol, e-numbers or drugs), and vitamin and mineral deficiencies. If your body isn't healthy and well-maintained, the 'wrong' chemicals and hormones can be produced, making you feel low — both mentally and physically. On the other hand, regular exercise and a good balanced diet will encourage the production and release of 'happy' chemicals like endorphins, which will make you an upbeat kind of being.

Conclusion: if you aren't looking after your body, you're not looking after your mind.

Something to do

Next time you feel down, go for a walk around the block with your mates, go swimming or do ten minutes of gentle aerobics.

But exercise is booor-ing!

I've always abhorred physical exercise. It's most probably a legacy from my school days when sport was limited to hockey (which in my opinion should be listed as a martial art) and athletics (jumping over sand-pits? No thanks). When you've spent three hours standing in hockey goal in sub-zero temperatures, or being laughed at because you can't run the five-minute mile backwards, then sport is associated with bad times, rather than good.

So here's the good news: not all physical activity is so unappealing. There's a chance that your school offers all sorts of non-competitive, non-traditional sports, like gymnastics, aerobics, synchronised swimming and dance. But even if your school is not yet

so forward-thinking, these are exactly the kinds of activities you'll find on offer in leisure centres all around the country.

We're growing up in what can only be described as the Pepsi-Max (registered trademark and all that) Generation of super-cool and highly-motivated people. We are supposed to have recognised that life is short and that every minute should be lived to limit. Because of this, new sports are being invented and old ones are being made more enticing. Take a look at this list and you'll see what I mean.

23 1/2 WICKED THINGS TO DO ON THE WEEKEND

Aerobics — don't go for the burn

I doubt if there is a hamlet in England that does not have its own aerobics class. So what's stopping you? Is it your footballer thighs? Lack of a suitably sexy bit of gear? Well, forget your shape and your outfit. The days of going for the burn, and comparing butt tightness are behind us. Aerobics has come gently of age.

Aquarobics — it's not wet, wet, wet

I know you think this is for old people and pregnant woman, but you're wrong. Marathon runners use aquarobics when warming up their muscles for a run. So you can just stop slagging off this extremely effective and kind-to-your-bod exercise right now.

BADMINTON — making a racquet indoors

This is always good for a laugh especially when all those Wimbledon wannabes have taken three swipes at the shuttlecock before it's even cleared the net. Chortle, chortle. Organise a large group and take over the indoor courts at the local leisure centre.

BOATING — go on, dip your oar

Depending on where you live, there's bound to be a lake, river or canal where it is possible to hire a boat or punt for a sedate Saturday afternoon row. Alternatively, enrol in a summer course (prices vary enormously, so phone around) where you can learn the basics of sailing and windsurfing. I hear that boys outnumber girls five to one in these courses. Enough said?

BOXERCISE — give it the old one-two

This has nothing to do with going 14 rounds in the ring, but everything to do with fitness. Boxercise consists of the warm-up exercises boxers do before they throw a punch. So find that old skipping rope and get jumping!

DANCING – strictly balls of fun

Go all hot and steamy with Latin American moves, tighten your stomach muscles with belly dancing, go Carmen with flamenco, or '50s mad with jive. Local further education groups usually include all manner of dance classes in their termly programmes and they're usually pretty inexpensive.

Football – good way to score

Most schools now have teams for both girls and boys, but if your enthusiasm is boundless you could follow the lead of 15-year-old Fiona of Nottingham. Fiona established her own football team, captained it, trained it and managed it. Watch out, Terry Venables.

Jogging — the footpath shuffle

Jogging has everything going for it. It's cheap, you can do it when you want and for as a long as you want. You can do it alone or pair-up with a friend. The only real outlay is a good pair of trainers to help absorb the impact when your feet hit the bitumen. Before you set out, warm up your muscles with some stretching

exercises. Then strap a Walkman to your waist, clamp those headphones in place, turn up the volume and go.

Kickboxing — the sport of supermodels

Kickboxing is a late-comer to trendy sports clubs, and the idea is that you flatten your opponent with a flick of your big, luridly-varnished toe-nail.

Mountain biking — hitting the trail

According to my mate Adele mountain biking was 'invented' at exactly the same time as *Charlie's Angels* hit the small screen, so it must be cool. It's piles more exciting than riding your kiddies' bike to and from school, and requires skill, stamina, a helmet and duvet-size protection pads. Though it would be nice to have your own wheels you can find holiday camps, both here and abroad, that hire out mountain bikes. Your local council will know of any specially-prepared bike trails in your area.

Pétanque — bowls with attitude

Sometimes called boule, this game originated in France, but has lately been attracting lots of attention in Britain. The aim is to get your steel balls closest to the coche, a small marker ball. It can be played in teams on any level gravelled surface, and even on the beach (use coloured plastic boule instead). To find a terrain near you, contact the British Pétanque Association in Coventry.

Power walking — you know, the fast one?

This is big, big, big in the States among woman-who-lunch, starlets and supermodels. Apparently the secret is in the hip and shoulder movement.

Riding — giddy-up

If you've never ridden a horse, it will take only a couple of lessons before you can go hacking with a group. There's no need to lash out and buy the pucker clobber, all you need is your least favourite pair of jeans and sturdy boots, and a county air. Not necessarily the cheapest diversion of them all, so add it to your Christmas or birthday present list.

Rollerblading — wheels on fire

In some cities blading is overtaking cycling as the fave mode of transport, especially among couriers. Thankfully, this hasn't meant the demise of bun-hugging Lycra shorts and cropped tops. There are in-line skates to suit all pockets, but whatever you do don't skimp on knee and elbow pads. Me, I'd also wear a helmet.

Scuba diving — baywatching from the bottom

Many local leisure centres offer introductory courses in scuba diving and you need travel no further than the nearest indoor swimming pool. Before instructors let you take your first underwater breath, they will teach you all the safety aspects and basic principles. If you prove a natural water-baby, you can enrol for further courses.

SNOWBOARDING — shooting the drifts

Some call it surf-on-snow, others think snowboarding is more akin to skateboarding. The only drawback is that it is a tad expensive — board, boots, bindings and waterproofs will set you back a couple of hundred quid. Ouch! It is possible to hire the equipment, and through the same outlet also enrol for lessons on a dry ski slope. For details on lessons contact your local council's leisure and amenities department, or any dry ski slope operation.

SQUASH — caught between four walls and a hard ball

It won't do you any harm to take some lessons before entering the court, but you can still enjoy this rocket-fast game as a complete novice. The rules are dead simple: avoid your partner's racquet, duck and dive if the ball is coming straight at you, and slam into the walls as gently as you can. Me, I also cower in the corner when the going gets tough. It is a good idea to wear a pair of special goggles when playing squash. These can be purchased at the court.

SURFING — bliss on a stick

Surfing was cool way before Keanu Reeves' near-naked portrayal of a wave-rider in the movie *Point Break*, and comes complete with its own culture: clothes, lingo, codes and babe boys. It's not the easiest skill to master (the trick's all in the paddling out, apparently), and you will need to beg or borrow a stick and find some water. But once you've got the knack it's a spiritual experience. What's more, it's a sport begging for more girl attention. One for the summer, huh?

Synchronised swimming — ballet with wet feet

Do it for fun with a group of friends, or take one of the many short courses offered at leisure centres during holidays. There are only two drawbacks with synchronised swimming: the singularly unattractive nose clip, and the enormous audience of boys it always attracts. Pity.

Trampolining — jumped up exercise

Now this is an easy one. All you've got to do is jump once and the trampoline does the rest. No wonder it's not an Olympic event. Strongly advise you don't wear a skirt!

Volleyball — dead cheap frenzy

An all-weather, all-comers sport (unless, like me, your arms bend backwards). All you need is a net or length of rope, something to tie the ends to, and a largish ball. It's best played on a soft surface, as all those dives aren't exactly kind to your bones. Volleyball is a huge State-side and Australian craze (You haven't see it on *Home and Away*?), and what's more, it's a strong, sexy-woman kind of sport.

W<small>ALL</small> C<small>LIMBING</small> — the only way is up

Apparently once you get into this, all other thrills pale in comparison. Unfortunately, this is not one you can do at home (parents take unkindly to holes being gouged in the living room wall), and you will have to make quite a few phone calls to locate your nearest 'wall'. But how do you get down? Abseil, of course.

Y<small>OGA</small> — the only exercise you can do sitting still

Not only will yoga increase your flexibility by gently encouraging your muscles to stretch, it will also give you inner calm. A great way to obliterate the stresses of the day, and prepare you mentally and physically for the next. Now say after me: Hummm.

See? Exercise doesn't have to be boring. So unless you want to become a professional couch potato with a stay-at-home life, then you'd be wise to participate. Oh, and by the way, did I mention that your love life could also benefit by getting out a bit more? The choice is yours — you can stay at home and watch *Blind Date* or you can go out and get a date.

TURNED ON MENTALLY

When you're at school your grey matter is always being exercised: tests to do, experiments to carry out, D&T stuff to design, and books to be read. But what happens when you get home? Zilch, zippo, nothing. School's sucked every ounce of initiative, leaving you inspirationally dead. You are so whacked you wouldn't recognise a good idea if it tripped you up in the hall.

To counter this, keep a diary and every time you have a brilliant idea for an outing or hobby, write it down. Then one day when you get home and are desperate for something to do, just refer to your directory of fun. There's bound to be something on your list that you can do there and then. Also keep a couple of pages free for recording awe-inspiring quotes.

SOMETHING TO DO

Pick a sport or activity that interests you, find out where you can do it and get some mates to go with you.

My Diary

RAVING, NOT MISBEHAVING

What's the most fun day you've had? Answers like reorganising your sock drawer, crimping your hair or having a lobotomy will not be accepted.

This month:

Month 2:

Month 3:

What new sports-like activities have you tried, or have made plans to try?

This month:

Month 2:

Month 3:

What differences have you noticed in your health and attitude?

This month:

Month 2:

Month 3:

chapter 6
LET'S INTERACT!
YOU GOTTA HAVE FRIENDS —
IT AIN'T NATURAL OTHERWISE

Good friends stop us being lonely. They're our soul-mates — the people with whom we share most of our growing-up experiences. They make us laugh, give us feedback (both welcome and unwelcome), are generous with love and support, give us the birthday presents we really want, help us, and kick us into place when we're out of it. They stop us going insane. My bestest mate Dave, when asked why we need friends, came up with this genius answer: "Well, could you imagine snowboarding alone? It wouldn't be natural." The superb thing about friendship is that it is a two-way street — we get a chance to return all this love and support to them. Like, it's better to give, than to receive. Agree?

Having friends is integral to the living process. Without friends how would we improve ourselves? We need objective opinions to keep ourselves in check.

For example, who else but a really good friend would tell you that you look a dag in a particular shirt? And who else but a really good friend would accept that, like it or not, you're going to continue wearing that daggy shirt because it's your favourite?

A lot of the good stuff we do, we do because of our friends. There's nothing nicer than getting the accolade of your friends for doing really well in a test, for getting a date with the guy you've been after for months, or for finally getting rid of that awful shirt. It's all well and good this self-improvement lark for self-satisfaction, but it feels an awful lot better when someone else appreciates your effort. Friends are as necessary as food and water. Friends? They're the real thing!

THE DIFFERENCE BETWEEN FRIENDS AND ASSOCIATES

You probably know a lot of people because you make an effort to talk to them. They might be the kids at school or those who live near you, people in the shops, your cousins or your parent's friends, the bus conductor or even the postman. If you counted all the bods you chat with frequently you'd be flabbergasted at the number.

But here's the thing: not all of those people are your friends, in fact very few could be counted as bosom buddies. Some of them hardly know you, nor you them; others you might know quite well, but not to the extent that you'd confide in them. Many of these associates (because that's what they really are) only know you at one level, like say, a teacher. Your teacher, though he or she might be quite friend-*ly*, isn't exactly a friend. For a start you only meet at school and you have no idea of his or her life away from the chalkface. No, a teacher might fulfil lots of the criteria I mentioned at the beginning of this chapter, but like the butcher, baker and candlestick-maker, a teacher is just an associate.

Friends are altogether more special. They are (she says, quickly grabbing a dictionary): Persons who feel mutual regard for another, sympathisers, helpers; people who are not enemies.

In our words friends:
+ like us for what we are;
◗ make an effort to understand us;
+ are nice to us (and when they're not it's for a good reason);
◗ sympathise with our problems and situations;
+ are there when we need help or a shoulder to cry on;
◗ are for us and not against us;
+ want to keep our company; and, most importantly,
◗ make an effort to share good times with us.

FRIEND OR FIEND?

Here comes the tricky bit! Sometimes, the people we call friends can have a pretty negative effect on us.

FILL IT IN!

MAKE A LIST OF ALL THE
PEOPLE YOU KNOW. PUT A
STAR NEXT TO THOSE WHO
ARE FRIENDS THROUGH THICK
AND THIN.

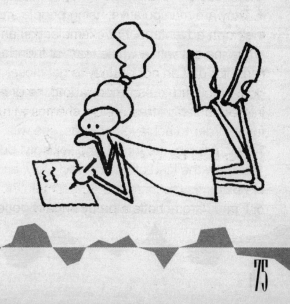

Sure, we have fun with them, they make an effort to understand us, they're nice to us (sometimes), and will occasionally do their all to help us. At times, though, they act more like enemies.

Now, everybody has their bad moments (yeah — you and me both) but that doesn't make them (or us) negative friends, just human. However, those guys who tend to bring you down most of the time, and deliberately or accidentally make you miserable are the ones you have to be wary of.

A FIENDISH GUIDE TO SPOTTING NEGATIVE FRIENDS

✦ They are always bitching, and you can be sure that if they slag off others, they'll do the same to you.

❱ They will go out of their way to distract you when they know you've important work to do.

✦ They are manipulative, using people and situations to their own advantage. For example: you and the fiend are going out with a whole team of friends, but for the fiend it is just an opportunity to get closer to her love god. The fiend doesn't care about the group, her only interest is self-interest. And if she has to ruin everyone's fun in order to achieve her ends, she will.

❱ Watch out for the friend who 'jokingly' puts you down. You know the kind of spiel: "Hey! Ugly, are you coming or not?"

✦ Fiends are not often the bearers of good news,

preferring either to ignore it, twist it or tell you an out-and-out porky pie. The way fiends work is like this: you were spotted in the street looking pretty glam by a mutual friend who mentions it to the fiend. When the fiend comes to tell you they forget the 'looking glam' bit and report only that so-and-so saw you. The professional fiend, will then turn on an expression of ultimate concern, look closely at your face and point out that there is a zit on the end of your nose.

▶ Fiends see the negative side of almost everything.

SOMETHING TO DO

Go through the list you made earlier and look at each of the starred names and cross off any who are negative friends. Remember, everyone has their off days and just because you've had a row with a mate, doesn't mean they're a fiend instead of a friend

FAREWELL MY FIEND

Now that you know how miserable negative friends can make you, it's time to work out ways of dealing with them.

1 You can avoid them.

2 If that's not possible, you should learn to take

everything they say with a pinch of salt. Don't let them put you down, or jeopardise your relationships with others.

3 Stand your ground. If they give you a hard time for doing well in an exam, just shrug your shoulders and make a joke about it. You mustn't allow them stop you doing what you want to do.

4 If all else fails, try to laugh off their bitchiness and negative thinking. No use wasting all your energy hassling with them.

You are in control of your life — and it's going to be a great one!

THE FRIENDSHIP PACT

1 Put in the effort to make friendships successful. All relationships have to be worked at.

2 Have fun by arranging to do things together. See pages 61-69 and 97-99 for ideas aplenty.

3 Don't get stuck into a routine of only seeing your friends at school, at the shops or the Friday night club. Break loose and let rip.

4 Learn to open up to your real friends.

5 Don't use friends as a way of meeting boyfriends or to go places.

6 Never abandon your friends for a boyfriend.

7 Make new friends but keep the old, 'cos one is silver and the other gold. A true friendship is not made overnight, it takes time.

8 Be honest. Don't tell your mates what they want to hear. Tell the truth and be considerate when doing so!

9 Be a good listener.

10 Stick up for your mates, and they'll do likewise.

My Diary

SOUL MATES

Write down the names of your closest, truest friends, and what makes them so.

Name:
Why:

Name:
Why:

Name:
Why:

Write down the names of three people you have met over the past few months, and say why you think they may become good friends.

Name:
Why:

Name:
Why:

Name:
Why:

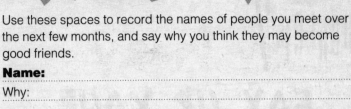

Use these spaces to record the names of people you meet over the next few months, and say why you think they may become good friends.

Name:

Why:

Name:

Why:

Name:

Why:

What have you done to improve the quality of your friendship?

This month:

Month 2:

Month 3:

What techniques have you used to cope with fiends? Put a star next to the most effective ones.

chapter 7

FOX UP YOUR FAMILY

IT'S TIME FOR A DOMESTIC BLITZ

You've just stepped in the door after a hard day at school, and even though your backpack weighs ten tonnes and you've enough homework to see you through to retirement, you're determined to be full of good cheer, and you're looking forward to some happy family banter. But what greets you isn't exactly a Waltons family welcome. Instead of the "Hi honey, nice day at school" repartee, you find your dad hopping up and down screaming about the hassles at work, and your mum is yelling because she has a headache. Alternatively, the only response to your "Hi, I'm home" could be the signature tune of *Neighbours*. Your family might just be one of those utterly, mind-numbingly boring ones where every week is a photostat of the one before: Monday, *Brookside;* Tuesday, *Eastenders;* Wednesday, Gran comes to tea;

Thursday, *Top of the Pops;* Friday, supermarket night; and Saturday is dad's day at the football and mum's day for catching up. Sunday is a lie- around and read-the-newspaper day. Boring!

Feel badly done by – well, wake up, you are witnessing family life real-world style. There is, however, hope on the horizon:

1 You will not have to endure this forever.

2 Your family does enjoy good times, it's just that you don't notice them.

3 Spreading the feel-good factor is easy. Beneath their scowls, your family is just itching for the good times.

4 YOU can put the *pop* back into you pa, the *mmmm* into your mum, and the *sssizzz* into your siblings. You can make with the domestic blitz.

LET'S FIZZ UP YOUR FAMILY

Legend has it that dutiful daughters and sons look to their parents for guidance in all matters. Usually this is true, but there are times when hard-working or stressed-out parents have to be kick-started into action by their sprogs. Sometimes, parents get so involved in the daily grind, they forget about having a life. They need you to remind them.

Hopefully, by this stage in *Get A Life!*, you'll have become a thoroughly active person with a very cool life. You'll understand that 'fun' is an attitude, not just a ticket to Alton Towers. If not, re-read chapter 1.

So how do you spread the gospel of fun to your family? You lead by example. Start by selecting a moment when your family are relaxed. There's no point trying to rally your mum into bungy jumping on the evening after her job appraisal. You have to take it slowly and lead them to full-blown fun inch-by-inch. Much better to start out with an easy activity that is not too threatening. For example, if your family is addicted to television, you could suggest doing the *Bamboozle* quiz in the Teletext Fun and Games section. That being successful, you could suggest that the next evening you play a board game (gasp) together (gasp, gasp).

It won't take long before suggestions of country walks and ice skating sessions are greeted with unanimous enthusiasm. For other *Get A Life!* ideas see pages 61-69. Who knows where family fun sessions might end up? The sky's the limit — parachuting, paragliding, moon walks!

Get the picture? A domestic blitz has to be done gradually. Rehabilitation can be a lengthy process, but it's worth the effort.

Once you've got a bit of action going down in the domicile, it's time to sort out those recurring hassles which can make home life hell. Time to reach for the **ten commandments** of domestic bliss.

THE TEN COMMANDMENTS OF DOMESTIC BLISS

1 *Thou shalt empathise*

Don't get mad with your mum for being in a mood. Care enough to take the time to ask what's bugging her. Remember, that her day at home or at work isn't a walk in the park. Listen, learn and try to see things from her perspective. If you try to understand her, she'll make more of an effort to understand you.

2 *Thou shalt do it without being asked*

Your room is a mess. You know it has to be tidied sooner or later, so make is sooner and save yourself a lecture about responsibility, growing up, etc, etc...

3 *Remindeth thy kin of the good times*

Every time your family does something really good together, dwell on it. Make a big deal of the positive stuff, and keep stumm about the negatives. By reminding them of a successful outing, you'll promote good feelings within everyone. If you convince them you are all one happy family, they will act accordingly.

4 Do unto thy sibling as thou would have them do unto you

This one is really simple: if you gripe at your sister for no reason, she'll do the same to you. Treat everyone well and you'll be treated well in return. Period.

5 Thou shalt retreat to a place of solitude and meditation

It's a good idea to give yourself a little bit of peace and quiet from your family when you need it. When you think things are about to explode — go a for a walk, take a long bath or even catch a quick nap. This time-out principle works, so tell your parents about it.

6 Thou shalt respect thy parents, and thy parents' parents...

Learn this and learn it now: rightly or wrongly, you cannot row with your parents. They are a responsible for you, and what's more they care deeply about you. Accept that some battles (like curfews, skin-piercing, and going to all-night raves) may never be won. And the battle itself could leave some nasty scars which may unnecessarily wreck your home-life.

7 Fuel not the fire of a family row

It's very difficult to fight with someone who won't be fought. If a member of your family is feeling hot-headed and vents their anger at you, make a strategic retreat. Calmly and politely walk away, and return only when they have simmered down and the issue can be discussed reasonably.

8 *Borrow only what is loaned and returneth it speedily*

This one is so obvious it needeth no explanation.

9 *Flattery getteth thou everywhere*

A bit of buttering-up never did anyone any harm. Tell your mum or dad when they are looking particularly ravishing/handsome/good enough to eat; praise your sister for high marks; and congratulate your brother if he scores at footie.

10 *Finally, forgetteth not that there is an Eastenders Omnibus on Sunday*

Dad, your hair looks amazing

If dad is threatening to ground you until the millennium because you're turned into 'The Square', and he wants to watch the news. Be diplomatic (and give yourself a chance for a social life) and give in. Let him be king of the air waves. The Vic can wait.

My Diary

FAMILY LIFE AND OTHER ADVENTURES

Write down four activities you could do with your family. Tick the ones you actually get around to trying.

This month:

1 .... **2** ....

3 .... **4** ....

Month 2:

1 .... **2** ....

3 .... **4** ....

Month 3:

1 .... **2** ....

3 .... **4** ....

How I put a stop to needless family bickering:

This month: ....

....

Month 2: ....

....

Month 3: ....

....

I have done the following jobs around the house without having to be told:

This month: ....

....

Month 2: ....

....

Month 3: ....

....

chapter 8

HANDLING THAT BOY THING

A LOVE STORY?

A true confession by Vici 'I was dumped' McCarthy.

His name was Paul. He thought he was something special, and so did I.

He used to sit at the back of my biology lab class, and all six feet of him oozed manliness. He was gorgeous from the top of his shiny blond hair to the bottom of his tanned feet. I was in love, but beyond discussing the importance of the endocrine system ("I think love is an emotion sparked by body chemicals. What do you think, Paul?") I don't think he even knew I existed.

Taking everything into consideration, I thought I was handling this unrequited love situation pretty well. Then, he snogged me.

Yup, Paul Cotton snogged me. He was having problems with his girlfriend, he said. He'd always liked me, he said. Loads of the boys liked me, he said. Would I go with him on a school trip, he asked. Like a lemming at a cliff, I jumped at the chance. Oh, yes I'd love to, I said.

It was the beginning of the end.

I went out with Paul for four weeks. His girlfriend – yes, she was still his real girlfriend – was going through agony. Meanwhile, I was spending every waking hour working out how I was going to keep Paul for my very own. I thought I'd die if he left me.

Then one mad, bad day he dumped me. I was gobsmacked. He gave me my marching orders unceremoniously on the back seat of the school bus. Everyone saw and heard the whole horrible performance. Paul told me he was getting together with his old girlfriend. I cried non-stop for 115 hours (ask my mum).

As much as I hated Paul for this whole sorry episode, I deserved the aggro. I had broken the golden girl rules:

1 I dated a boy with a girlfriend. Bad move.

2 I showed no self-respect. I should have told Paul that I don't go out with other girls' boyfriends.

3 I put my life on hold for him. I spent a whole term hanging around the phone, waiting for him to call.

Now that I'm older (quite a lot) and wiser (just a little), I've worked out a code of conduct which girls should follow when dealing with the opposite sex. Stick

to the code, and your love life will be relatively painless. Forget it, and you're asking for trouble. It takes courage and self-respect to live within the code, but girls have these characteristics in abundance.

THE VICI CODE OF CONDUCT

1 Respect yourself

Boys respect girls who respect themselves. Self-respect glows like a beacon, so if you can see the beauty in yourself, everyone will see it. If you picture yourself as a dim, ugly hag, you'll act accordingly and people will avoid you like the plague.

2 Don't take rejection personally

If a guy doesn't like you, that's his problem. Why should you fret and accumulate worry lines about it? His appalling taste is a reflection on him, not you.

If you were to question a random selection of 50 men and ask them whether they fancied Meg Ryan, 20 would say "Cor! Phwoargh! Absolutely!"; ten would give a lukewarm response ("Oh yeah, she's all right."), and another 20 would say "Er, ta, but no. Not really into Meg." Now should Meg be feeling down and contemplating entering a nunnery? Of course not.

What one man loves, another man detests. (I hate baked beans, Snowboarding Dave lives on them.) If a boy doesn't fancy you, it's not because you're hideous, too smart, too tall, too pimply — you're simply not his type. And for that matter, he's most probably not yours either. Don't try to remake yourself to become 'his type'. Be proud of the original and unique you.

I know it sounds trite, but there is a relationship with your name on it somewhere. It might not be in biology lab class, nor on the school bus, so don't waste precious time sweating over it. My final words on this are: dump the rejection depression.

3 Accept nothing but the best

Before you can discover the mate of your dreams, you need to decide what you want. You'd be surprised at how many people fall into a relationship without really knowing if that's the one they want. Granted, we all make mistakes, but once you've realised your error don't hang around in the relationship out of habit, or because you're scared of being alone. Don't go for second best baby, or it'll be doomed right from the start. For the ultimate know-what-you-want on the love front, do the quizzes on pages 94, 96, 101 and 103.

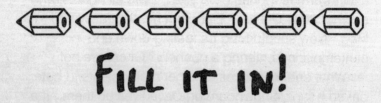

FILL IT IN!

Write down the name of a boy who has dumped you, and try to remember how you reacted.

Would you regard your behaviour at that time as a true reflection of your character? A simple yes or no will do.

4 Don't put your life on hold

If you live and die by the phone, then it's time for a radical change, and **D.I.N**. (Re-read chapter 3 for a pep-talk on 'doing-it-now'.)

Time is precious and your life is the most valuable thing you have, so don't waste it camping by the telephone waiting for *that* call. As of now, phone loitering without purpose is a criminally insane offence.

If a boy wants to get in touch with you, he will find a way. Parents (and even brothers and sisters) will take messages, and, of course, he could always send you a letter. Ah, so romantic.

Now that you have a whole heap of free time, reclaim your life. Do things, get ahead with your study or laugh until ye can laugh no more. And if the blighter still hasn't rung (not that you've really had time to notice), accept that he isn't the right person for you. Poor soul doesn't know what he's missing.

5 Try not to be boy mad

No matter how much you'd like to have a boyf, please remember that you can live without one. Being boy-mad will get you nowheresville. Boys, for all their shortcomings, can sense when a girl is desperate, and they do not find it attractive. Turning into a slimy, giggly heap of ooze every time a love god comes near is a symptom of flagging self-respect. But if you ooze self-respect, others (including boys) will be honoured that you've deigned to keep with them.

Upon noticing the first twinges of desperation in yourself, quietly chant this mantra: "I am the centre of my universe. I am able to have a brilliant time on my own. I do not need some guy to make me complete and to help me enjoy life." Although, that's not to say I wouldn't be the tiniest bit thrilled if a cool guy turned up *mumble, mumble, mumble...*

The other thing about being boy-mad is that it drives your parents berserk. Now I know that's fun sometimes, but it also means they'll come down on you like a tonne of bricks when it comes to dating. You're also leaving yourself wide open for loooooong lectures.

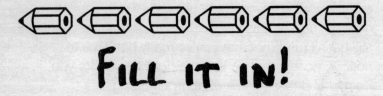

FILL IT IN!

Think of a time when you have put your life on hold for a boy and write it here. Should you have done it? What did you gain?

Was it worth it? A simple yes or no will do.

Would you do it again? Yes or no?

6 Don't be afraid to make mistakes

This is one that I always tend to forget. Jumbled among the sensible calculations of whether a guy is right for me or not, I often tend to cut boys out of my life because they might not be perfect and I might end up with a broken heart. Even if a relationship does go sour, something positive does comes out of it. It's good to know that you can feel such deep emotion, because it is that same emotion that allows you to be committed to a cause, to a friend, or to a secret ambition. A mistake in any endeavour, whether it be love or classroom tests, is a dress rehearsal for the real thing.

The Making Mistakes Secret is simply this: don't be afraid to really love someone — it can only be a positive thing.

SOMETHING TO DO

HOW TO SPEND QUALITY TIME WITH YOUR GUY

Found a boy you can 'work' with? Think you've got the basics of a happening thing? Great stuff. Here are a few suggestions for spending quality time together.

▶ Go to the cinema. It may not be the most private, but at least you can get good popcorn.

✦ Go ten-pin bowling. He may not be bowled over by your gutter balls, but your sense of fun will inevitably score a strike. Groan, groan.

◗ People watch. Install yourselves on a bench in a busy public place and invent fictional lives for the people who pass by.

✦ Go to the beach whatever the weather. Beaches are always romantic.

◗ Plan the perfect holiday. Go to a travel agent, select a couple of brochures and plan a very expensive make-believe holiday. You may not be able to travel together, but you can certainly dream together.

✦ Go play on the swings. The world looks a lot different when you're reinacting *Apollo 13* on a kiddie swing. But whatever you do, don't menace the junior set when they come to play.

◗ Hit the kitchen and cook. This little activity serves two purposes. Firstly, it lets him know where you stand when it comes to gender stereotyping. And, secondly, you can concoct a truly romantic dinner pour deux .

✦ Go to the footie. Believe it or not there's something very intimate about sharing a hot pie and a cold bench in the middle of winter surrounded by thousands of people. Oh, and by the way, the footie's not bad either.

◗ Give each other a manicure or pedicure. Now there's no need for all that guffawing. The beauty about this little number is that it provides the perfect opportunity for a deep and meaningful conversation. Trust me, I know what I'm talking about.

✦ Get love on the run by planning a get fit routine together. For example, meet for a short jog (not snog) before or after school, and on weekends arrange to work out together in the gym followed by 40 laps of the swimming pool. (For other action girl and boy ideas see chapter 5.) Forget the competitive boy versus girl aspect, and instead concentrate on improving your combined performances. This is surely the way to beat the loneliness of the long distance runner.

SHOPPING FOR LOVE

Grab your hat, Gertie, we're going on a mental shopping trip!

Imagine that we're in the town centre and you want to buy a coat that will last you for ages. You're going to invest a lot in this coat, so you're going to take great care in choosing the right one.

First, you keep your cash safe so no one can steal it, then you shop around and try on a few coats. You've decided the style you want, it's just a matter of closely checking the fit and the quality. Finally, at the end of the day you decide whether you've seen a coat you want. If not you take your money home and wait until another day. You don't settle for an-also ran, a second-best.

So enlighten me about why it is that all this effort and care is expended when buying clothes, and not a tenth of it when choosing a boyfriend? Don't know? Me neither! A lot of girls don't value or care enough about the love they've got to give — and they let themselves be ripped off. Some girls haven't a clue what they're looking for in a boyfriend (or a coat for that matter), so spend ages with totally unsuitable ones. Some girls think they've found *the* boy, or one that will do for the moment, and leap headlong into the relationship without really checking it out.

So here's what we're going to do in this filly-in bit: we're going to stop you from being either a compulsive or impulsive shopper for boys.

FILL IT IN!

What kind of boy do you want?

What kind of relationship are you after? How will you get to know someone properly before taking the plunge and saying "I wuv you"?

How will you make certain you're not giving your love to simply anyone who asks?

IS THAT ALL THERE IS TO IT?

It surely is. Show self-respect and discretion and all this love stuff will be easier.

Of course, you don't need a boyfriend. One of the great one-liners of the women's liberation movement is: A woman needs a man like a fish needs a bicycle. You might not want or even be ready for a relationship. Great, so go party!

MY DIARY

I LOVE HIM, I LOVE HIM NOT

Write down the name of some boys who interest you (if there are any) and say why. What are their good and gross points?

Name:

Why:

Good   Gross

Name:

Why:

Good   Gross

Name:

Why:

Good   Gross

In what ways have you put into practice the Vici Code of Conduct?

This month:

Month 2:

Month 3:

Write down some boy-truths you have learnt.

chapter 9

BEATING THE CLASS SYSTEM

Is SCHOOL A BLUR OR AN OASIS?

Try to forget all the stereotype images of school. You know the stuff: a nightmare from hell populated by devilish teachers eager to inflict pain, and as hip as the ancient Egyptians they're so mad about.

Forget it all. It's just not true. Though I can't vouch for all your teachers, I can promise you that the ancient Egyptians were mighty fine people. They were well into astrology, knew how to whip up a potent zit-zapper, and invented the predecessor to your Swatch. (Their sand and water clocks went drip drop, not tick tock.) While the Egyptians were building pyramids, and discussing the intricacies of herbal medicine, we Brits were living in hovels, saying "Uba, uba, uba".

But here's something you might not like about the Egyptians: they invented school. The horror started when some bright soul drew a picture and then gave his doodle a meaning. For instance, a wavy line could mean water. Not content, he went on to create symbols to represent sounds. There was no stopping the Egyptians now — if you could say it, they could write it. Hieroglyphics (and shopping lists) had been invented!

The next good idea was to teach children to use hieroglyphics, and to do this they opened scribal schools. One thing led to another, and before long the curriculum included maths, science, history and drawing. So you see, one man's doodle led to your local comprehensive. Scary, huh?

Do we hate the Egyptians? Course not. Getting an education is crucial if you want to fulfil your dreams. If you dream of 52-room palaces and exotic hols, there's little chance of getting them if you're on the dole with no prospects of a job or career. To make school an oasis, not a blur, read on.

scribal Comprehensive

WHAT NOT TO DO IN SCHOOL

Sometimes we are our own worst enemy. We turn school into a torture trap. In essence all that we are required to do at school is:

1 Attend

2 Pay attention

3 Do homework and hand it in on time

4 Understand and learn what we're taught

5 Sit exams

But what many of us do is abandon this simple five-point agenda, and replace it with this monster:

1 Occasionally bunk classes and when we do attend, arrive late and thus peeve our teachers.

2 Fail to pay attention during class and incur the wrath of the teacher when we ask dumb questions later.

3 Don't do homework and...

4 Spend a lot of time in detention.

5 Get the grumps because nothing ever goes right: we're always in strife, do our work badly, get low marks, and are ear-bashed by anxious parents.

6 The poor marks make us feel stupid so we become more discouraged. Our work becomes shoddier and is handed in even later.

7 Don't bother revising because we've convinced ourselves we are stupid and won't get any questions right no matter how much study we do.

8 Go through the terror of exams knowing full well we haven't revised.

9 Fail exams.

10 Get grief from everybody about doing badly.

11 Punish ourselves with a case of the guilts because we're not exactly thrilled at our prospects for the future.

Who can break this terrible chain reaction? YOU!
You have the power to smooth your academic journey,
and to make learning and understanding your subjects
a tad more interesting. In some areas you can
transform hell into heaven overnight (for example,
doing your homework as soon as it is given), but in
others the benefits take time. For example, to get a
handle on Shakespeare's lingo will require more than a
quick skim. Keep at it. The hard work will pay off.

A YEARNING FOR LEARNING

Look it up

If you're reading a passage from a text book and you
suddenly realise that it's not making any sense, the
chances are you've misunderstood a word or phrase.

For instance, you may have read that 'Henry VIII
adored the canticle' and assumed a canticle was a
jacket, when in actual fact it is a hymn. If you continued
reading and found out that Hank was into singing,
you'd be pretty muddled. "What the jiggins has an
anorak got to do with rapping?" you'd ask.

So before you read another word, go back over the
material, find the offending words and look them up in a
dictionary. Once you're thoroughly au fait with the
meaning, you can press on with the rest of text.

Ask questions

You know the meaning of all the difficult words and

have re-read the text, but you still can't make head or tail of it. What should you do?

a De-de-defer!

b Ask your teacher for help

If you chose 'b', you're on the right track. Helping is what teachers are paid (though not nearly enough) to do. I know some of us believe that teachers are government spies, secreted into our classrooms to suss out prospective criminals and *Take That* fans, but — as the child of two teachers — I can promise you that the professors of the classroom chose their career because they really want to educate. (Of the two teachers I surveyed, only one occasionally delighted in embarrassing *Take That* fans.) So next time you get stuck on something, don't just skip over it hoping that one day you'll understand it, ask the teacher to make it crystal clear — and **D.I.N**!

Learn as you go

If you want to make studying really easy for yourself, learn as you go. It's much easier to learn and memorise stuff that is fresh in your mind than material you covered in class seven weeks ago. Learning like this also takes the stress out of examination time, because you can devote yourself to revising, not learning everything from scratch.

You've read the book — now see the film

If you're having trouble grasping a topic, try a multi-media approach. Textbooks and school notes are fine, but they aren't the be-all and end-all. Find alternative sources of enlightenment in TV and radio programmes, (most newspapers give a special listing of educational-type programmes), newspapers (certain editions carry terrific study supplements), audio tapes and videos. Don't forget you can borrow tapes from your local library, and a staff member will be only too happy to arrange an inter-library borrowing for special books. Like teachers, librarians are there to help. Just because you can't make a racket in the library, it doesn't mean you can't start up a conversation with the librarian.

The multi-media approach works a treat if you're doing the Bard. On the page, Bill's banter can seem like a foreign language with all that olde worlde English, but if you hire an audio or video tape (like Zeffirelli's *Romeo and Juliet*) or, better still, cough up the cash to see a live production, Shakespeare will suddenly make sense. You'll see what he's on about, and realise that he was a pretty clued-up bloke. Remember that when Bill put pen to paper to write his plays, they were meant to be performed. He didn't expect anyone to sit in a quiet corner and read them.

Another example: I'm dreadful at French, so whenever possible, I buy French magazines loaded with articles that really interest me. For example, when I find a story on Keanu (phwoargh!) I sit down with a French grammar book and dictionary beside me, and plough through the article word by word, phrase by phrase until I've got the nitty-gritty. Well, a girl's gotta know what Keanu thinks about Pamela Anderson. C'est mega-grand important, non?

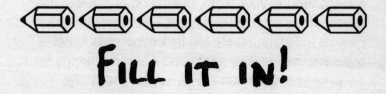

Fill it in!

Draw it instead

This one might raise a few eyebrows with your folks who won't see any connection between drawing and studying, but without a doubt this is one of the most effective ways of remembering. You know the saying: A picture paints a thousand words.

If you get particularly stuck on a topic, for example the factors that contribute to the green-house effect, get out your felt-tips and draw a picture that includes all the relevant information. Your doodle might feature a burning light bulb and some little pink monsters called Chloro Fluoro Carbons chomping at the ozone. When you come to recall it for a test, the picture will come to mind and the answer will be at your fingertips, so to speak.

Go on, be teacher for a day

To check that you know something thoroughly, pretend to teach it to somebody else. I'm deadly serious! Once you think you've learned a topic inside out, take on the role of teach and impart all you know onto a v. cool person (welcome back Keanu!) This may involve talking out loud, answering imaginary questions, walking around your room, illustrating examples on sheets of paper, and picking on *Take That* fans. Your parents will immediately call for the persons in white coats to come and take you away — but what the heck. If you can't explain something to your imaginary student, then go back to your books; you obviously don't know the subject well enough! Shame on you.

Rhyme time

Poems, limericks and rhyming couplets are great ways of remembering tricky facts and figures, so if you get a mental block about dates (numerical, not social) or mathematical formulae, give rhyming a go and see if it works. This is the rhyme I made up so I could remember when *Eastenders* started: In nineteen hundred and eighty-five, Albert Square became alive. Okay, so I won't be giving up my day job, but do I ever forget this significant date? Never. And nor will you.

First letters only

If you have a list of associated names to remember, take the first letter of each and create a word. For instance: the composition of water is hydrogen and oxygen = WHO. And for those doing German here is a way of remembering prepositions taking the accusative case: **d**urch, **o**hne, **g**egen, **w**ider, **u**m, **f**ür, **e**ntlang spells DOGWUFE. Now who could forget that?

Catchy phrases

Lists can also be memorised by taking the first letter of each word and turning them into a catchy phrase. For example: the layers of the earth's atmosphere (troposphere, stratosphere, mesosphere, ionosphere, exosphere) can be remembered by the phrase: Two silly men in England.

Picture links

If you are learning a language or are trying to remember the meaning of obscure or confusing English words, use mental pictures to link the word to its meaning. For instance, in Japanese, 'ahiru' means duck, so create a mental image of a duck transforming into 'a hero' donned in Superman-type garb.

Something to do

Here are six words, some foreign, for which you can create picture links.

phalanges (bones of the fingers or toes)

metamorphosis (to change)

die Tasse (German for 'the cup')

entlausen (German for 'getting rid of vermin')

aussi (French for 'also')

panne (French for 'breakdown')

Something else to do

Close your eyes and make a movie about something you have learnt in a recent history lesson. Give your favourite actor or actress the lead role and create a script based on the historical facts. Don't try to include absolutely everything, just pick out the important stuff.

Animate it!

It's much easier to recall a picture, especially an animated one, than a word, so when you're struggling to remember something complicated turn it into a movie or animated cartoon.

The only way I could ever get baobab trees in the right soil type was to imagine the tree as a bottle (baobab trees are bottle-shaped) leaking warm red wine into the soil. The association between this and the fact that baobab trees are found in iron-rich — red-coloured — soils in warm tropical climates is unforgettable.

A hint: make your movies really weird. The weirder they are, the easier they'll be to remember! You'll never forget that the potato and tobacco were discovered during Queen Elizabeth I's time if you imagine the esteemed red-head juggling potatoes while smoking a a fat cigar.

Number-word code

A bit tricky this one, because before you can use it you have to rote-learn a rhyming number-word list:

1= bun　　　　　　**6= sticks**

2= shoe　　　　　　**7= heaven**

3= tree　　　　　　**8= gate**

4= door　　　　　　**9= sign**

5= beehive　　　　**10= hen**

Once memorised, apply it to those must-remember dates. Let's say you're trying to remember that King Harold died in the Battle of Hastings in 1066. Imagine a battle in full flow, Harold dead on his back with an arrow in his eye, and a hen beside him carrying two sticks. The hen represents ten, and the two sticks stand for 66. Put it all together and you get 1066.

SOMETHING TO DO

Use the number-word code to create images for these significant dates:

442 (the last Roman troops left Britain, burying their gold so that no one could find it)

1588 (Spanish Armada set sail for England)

1903 (Emmeline Pankhurst founded the Suffragettes)

1914 (start of World War 1)

So, DOING WELL AT SCHOOL IS THAT EASY HUH?

Not quite, but almost. Just as in every aspect of our lives, we excel in some things and not others, it's the same at school. Some kids are academically tuned-in and have no problem getting good exam results, some are highly co-ordinated making them good sportspeople, while others are a whiz at hands-on stuff. Some bods are very creative and imaginative which means that story-writing or D&T are their forte.

What you have to remember is that everyone is good at something. As long as you do justice to your strengths, develop your attributes, and put extra effort into the 'yuk!' subjects, you stand an excellent chance of succeeding in the career of your choice. Dream on!

BE YOUR OWN CAREERS COUNSELLOR

Before you start this section get hold of a careers dictionary from your school or local library, and re-read chapter 2 of *Get A Life!* to plug in to your goals.

Making your mind up about a career is never easy, so most people try to postpone it as long as possible. At the beginning of high school you'll hear the Dilly Defer-Agains say: "Er, I'll wait until I do my GCSEs before I decide." And with them done, they will defer again until the A levels are finished. Same thing at university. And then before you know it the degree is completed and the Dillies are taking a year off. At the ripe old age of 23 they finally decide to be zoo-keepers, but unfortunately have all the qualifications to be ships' technicians. These bods left the planning a little too late. Even if you don't want to go on to further education, you still have to chose your subjects carefully, so that you have the most suitable background for the job of your choice.

Though you don't have to decide right about your future, it might be an idea to start thinking of the broad area in which you'd like to work. At least with something in mind, you'll avoid the pitfalls of dropping subjects that will prove vital later on.

Money, money, money

This is all about making sure that your career can 'pay' for your lifestyle dream. Let's say, for example, you want to work for an environmental charity which involves lots of travelling. Nice one! You also want a big house and a big family. You may have a problem.

This job may not be very well paid. Can you afford a large house? And all that travelling may make having a large family impossible. Will there be enough dosh to take your children with you or pay for someone to look after them at home? Would you want to be away from your family for long periods? Just because your plan has a few hiccups, don't abandon it, you may just have to compromise here and there.

FILL IT IN!

Ask yourself what you're good at (not just subjects at school, but other things too, like your hobbies), then look through a careers dictionary. List jobs which match your interests and skills.

Subjects I'm good at:

Hobbies and interests:

Jobs which use my strengths:

Now write down some careers that really inspire you, and alongside list the prerequisite subjects.

Job: **Subjects needed:**

Job: **Subjects needed:**

Job: **Subjects needed:**

Think about how you want your job to fit into your dream lifestyle. Do you want a career that lets you travel? Are you an office person or would you prefer to work from home?

My Diary

COURSES FOR ACTION

How have you made school easier for yourself?
This month:
....
....
....

Month 2:
....
....

Month 3:
....
....

What learning techniques have you used successfully?
This month:
....
....

Month 2:
....
....

Month 3:
....
....

Have you had any second thoughts about your dream life?
This month:
....
....

Month 2:
....
....

Month 3:
....
....
....

chapter 10

GIVING A LITTLE BACK
WELCOME TO THE WORTHY BIT

This is where we're all supposed to get very serious, look ourselves straight in the eye (metaphorically, of course — it's difficult without a mirror) and say in stern voice: "So, what are you doing for the planet, buddy?" You are going to listen to the good angel on your right shoulder, ignore the devil on the left and acquire a conscience. Like you need another one, OK? No one would blame you if you tuned out, stared at the wall, and started to understand the merits of listening to your Dad's old *Genesis* records, but that would be a truly desperate act. I know there is not much street-cred to be earned from wanting to help people. I accept that some of your peers may give you a hard time. To be thought of as 'nice', is tantamount to being twinned with Cliff Richard. Sexy it's not!

EMPOWERMENT TO THE PEOPLE!

But there is another way of looking at do-gooding, and that is to see it as empowering. Helping someone gain control over their life is to empower them, and in this chapter you're going to learn that YOU have the power to empower. And whatever you might think about do-gooding, empowering isn't boring and it's damn sexy.

If you're on the floor, rolling around in hysterical laughter, and thinking that this Vici-woman should lighten up, I really can't blame you. My philosophy of life can be attributed to my pseudo-hippie upbringing. (Send letters of complaint/support to the publishers, marked for the attention of The Author's Mum and Dad.) Here follows the McCarthy Philosophy of Life:

What goes around, comes around

Many people, including me, believe that what you do comes back to haunt you or reward you. It's called the law of Karma. Karma works on a cause and effect basis. If you're nice to someone, they'll be nice in return. You tell someone a lie, you'll be found out in the end. To sum up: what goes around, comes around.

IF NOT YOU, THEN WHO?

For good things to be done, good people have to do them. If a wall desperately needs to be pulled down (like the one between East and West Germany), someone needs to remove the first brick before the heavies can come in with the bulldozers.

There are too many people who moan constantly about all the bad stuff going down in the world, but aren't prepared to do fig about it. They believe that someone else will do it, and pretend that they wouldn't be of help even if they did get involved. If everyone thought the same then nothing would ever be changed for the better. So something else for you to ponder upon: If you don't do something, who will?

YOU WERE PROBABLY BORN UNDER A LUCKY STAR

I was talking about this part of the book with a friend, and she said I was playing the heavy. She thought I was shouldering responsibility onto people who have plenty enough to worry about, without worrying about others. "Let's face it," she said, "everyone creates their own destiny, so why should your readers be worried about the homeless, the poor *blah, blah, blah* who do nothing to help themselves." But that's not how I see the issue of caring and sharing.

The homeless and the poor did not choose to live that way, they had no choice. Street kids may have left homes in which they were abused; the poor may have been born in countries where poverty affects all but the few. These people are not poor because they are lazy or unmotivated, or homeless because they like it.

On the other hand, many of us were born under a lucky star and were raised in secure and comfortable homes. We are no more deserving of the good life than anyone else. So isn't it up to us to be thankful, and in return give a little back to those who weren't so lucky?

I accept that this is an unfashionable concept, but one worth thinking about. You may agree or disagree with my ideas, so forward your letters of complaint/support to the publishers, okay?!

ARE YOU GOING TO DO SOMETHING TO MAKE THE WORLD A BETTER PLACE?

Everyone can do their bit to make the globe a little more positive. You don't have to be Director General to the United Nations or Wonder Woman to do it. You don't need to be super-fit or super-brainy or super-together at all! You don't have to chain yourself to a whaling boat or board a plane to the nearest Third World country. Good stuff can be achieved with the tiniest bit of energy. Writing a letter to the council about the appalling state of the kids' playground, or about the dangerous crossing you have to make on your way to school are a start. And, yes, even turning off unnecessary lights and recycling bottles can have big positive consequences.

Here are a few ideas which you can put into action at home or in the wider community. Don't be a Lone Ranger, recruit friends to help; it will make the going easier and the fun-level greater. And if you recall the law of Karma, every effort you make, will improve not only the lot of someone else, but also your own.

Doing it for friends and family

1 Act as a peace-keeper and smooth out misunderstandings between rowing parties. Pass on positive comments and toss the negative ones in the bin.

2 Help members of your family who are stressed-out. In return there will be fewer fights, and a peaceful environment will be maintained.

3 Make 'em laugh, make 'em laugh, make 'em laugh. What would the world be like without a few jesters?

Doing it for the community

1 Contact your local hospital to find out if they are running a fund-raising campaign to purchase a special piece of equipment. If they are, entreat your friends and family to help raise money.

2 Organise a recycling collection rota in your street.

3 Arrange to pop-in for a chit-chat with an elderly pensioner in your neighbourhood.

DOING IT FOR EVERYONE

1 Knowledge is power. Learn about different cultures, and spread the word about tolerance.

2 Perhaps you might like to join an organisation like Amnesty International (0171 814-6200). Amnesty members write letters to governments expressing concern about the abuse of human rights (for example, false imprisonment and torture) in their countries. All you need is a pen, a piece of paper, an envelope, a stamp, and you could save a person's life.

3 Be positive and laugh a lot. It's terribly contagious, and could turn someone's miserable day upside-down.

DOING IT FOR THE PLANET

1 Make your house environmentally-friendly. Knock the thermostat down a couple of degrees, give the flick to burning lights, don't buy anything with CFCs, be careful when disposing of corrosive or poisonous liquids, and say "no" to plastic shopping bags.

2 Buy a few plants, plant them (!) and look after them.

3 Join a pro-environment charity, like The World Wide Fund for Nature (01483 426-444), Friends of the Earth (0171 490-1555) or Greenpeace (0171 354-5100).

My Diary
LifE — Living And Loving
it

Write down one thing you've done on the do-good front.
This month:

Month 2:

Month 3:

Pen a slogan which you can use to keep your spirits up while you fight the good fight.
This month:

Month 2:

Month 3: